Kimly Craig Publicat

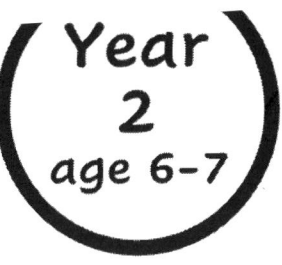

**Year 2**
age 6-7

**Adventure Stories**

# Creative Writing for Children

Supporting the English National Curriculum writing and spelling objectives for Key Stage 1

# List of titles by Kimly Craig Publications

## Creative Writing for Children

(published in February 2022)

Adventure Stories for age 6-8
Adventure Stories for Y2

\* \* \* \* \*

(coming soon in 2022)

Adventure Stories for Y3
Adventure Stories for Y4
Adventure Stories for Boys
Adventure Stories for Girls

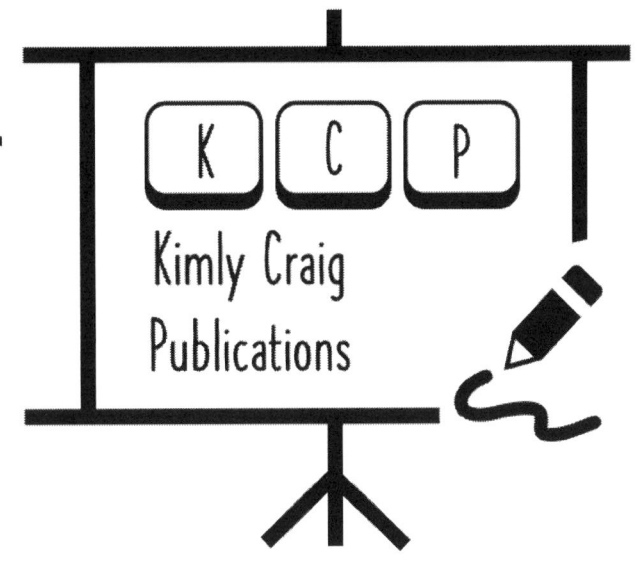

Kimly Craig
Publications

 kimly.craig.publications@gmail.com

 Certificate on its way!

To celebrate your child's achievement, email us their first name with a copy of their finished story and we will send back a personalised certificate to print out.

Write "Certificate" and your child's first name in the subject line and the certificate will be on its way!

# A Note for Adults

## Learning to Write

Learning to write is an essential life skill that your child will begin to acquire from the very first day at school. Strong writers will be well equipped for any future direction in life.

## Skillset

There are many skills for your child to master on their journey to becoming a strong writer, including letter formation, handwriting, accurate spelling and punctuation. While this can at times seem daunting, there are lots of ways to help your child achieve success.

## Practice and Enjoyment

Regular practice is key for all children to reach their potential as competent writers and if we can find ways for them to enjoy the process of writing, this can only help. Each story starter in this book is designed to fire your child's imagination. There are also specific spelling words to practise as well as boxes for them to create illustrations and a book cover.

## Your Role

Your role in ensuring your child's progress in writing cannot be underestimated. Correcting errors in spelling and punctuation is certainly important but remember that Rome wasn't built in a day and that not all mistakes need to be fixed immediately. Taking time to talk through ideas with your child before they start their story will be invaluable and encouraging them to share their story with loved ones will also support their growing confidence. If you would like to email us the story your child is most proud of, we will email you back a personalised certificate to print out for them to celebrate their achievement.

# A Note for Children

## Adventure Stories

This book has fifteen story starters for adventure stories that we really hope you are going to enjoy writing.

## What are Common Exception Words?

Common Exception Words are words that are tricky to read and even trickier to spell. To help you learn them, we have included five of these words in the introduction to each story. Will you be able to include all five of them in the rest of the story when you write it?

## Instructions

1. Begin by completing the tracing activity for the story that you are going to write.
2. Complete the spelling grid activity. First read the word, then cover it up and practise writing it. Only look at it again if you need to.
3. Read the story starter and discuss it with someone who can help you. Think about how you are going to complete the story.
4. Write your story and remember to include the five common exception words for that story. Don't forget to check your spelling.
5. In the small boxes, draw pictures and in the large one, design a cover for your story. Imagine that you are writing a real book!
6. When you have finished your story, there is a wordsearch and colouring activity page to reward you for all your hard work.
7. Remember to colour in the cupcakes on your reward chart for each of the story activities you complete.
8. Finally, choose your best story and ask an adult to email it to us. We will email back a certificate to print out and show everyone!

# Common Exception Words

## Year 1

| | |
|---|---|
| a | some |
| are | **the** |
| ask | there |
| **be** | they |
| by | to |
| **come** | today |
| **do** | **was** |
| **friend** | we |
| full | were |
| **go** | where |
| **has** | **you** |
| he | your |
| here | |
| his | **Please note:** |
| house | Year 1 |
| **I** | spellings are |
| is | here for |
| **love** | reference |
| **me** | only and are |
| my | not a focus |
| **no** | within this |
| **of** | book. |
| one | Children in |
| once | Year 2 will |
| our | hopefully be |
| **pull** | able to |
| push | correctly |
| put | spell all |
| **said** | Year 1 words |
| says | but continual |
| school | reinforcement |
| she | is essential. |
| so | |

## Year 2

| | |
|---|---|
| **after*** | hour |
| again | **improve** |
| any | **kind** |
| **bath** | **last** |
| beautiful | **many** |
| because | mind |
| behind | money |
| both | most |
| break | move |
| busy | Mr |
| **child** | Mrs |
| children | **old** |
| Christmas | only |
| class | **parents** |
| climb | pass |
| clothes | past |
| cold | path |
| could | people |
| **door** | plant |
| **even** | poor |
| every | pretty |
| everybody | prove |
| eye | should |
| **fast** | steak |
| father | sugar |
| find | sure |
| floor | **told** |
| **gold** | **water** |
| grass | who |
| great | whole |
| **half** | wild |
| hold | would |

*Highlighted words: tricky spellings used in the stories in <u>this</u> book.

# My Book of
# Adventure Stories

Name: _____

Age: _____

# Contents

Reward Chart for stories 1 - 5

1. The Best Snow Day Ever

2. A Trip to the Circus

3. A Walk in the Forest

4. Grandad's Greenhouse

5. A Day at the Water Park

Reward Chart for Stories 6 - 10

6. The Talking Tree

7. My Summer Holiday

8. The Friendly Robot

9. A Naughty Dog

10. Buried Treasure

Reward Chart for Stories 11 - 15

11. Tom's New Tree House

12. A Day in Candyland

13. Fun at the Park

14. The Magic Jigsaw

15 The Lost Little Elf

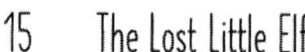

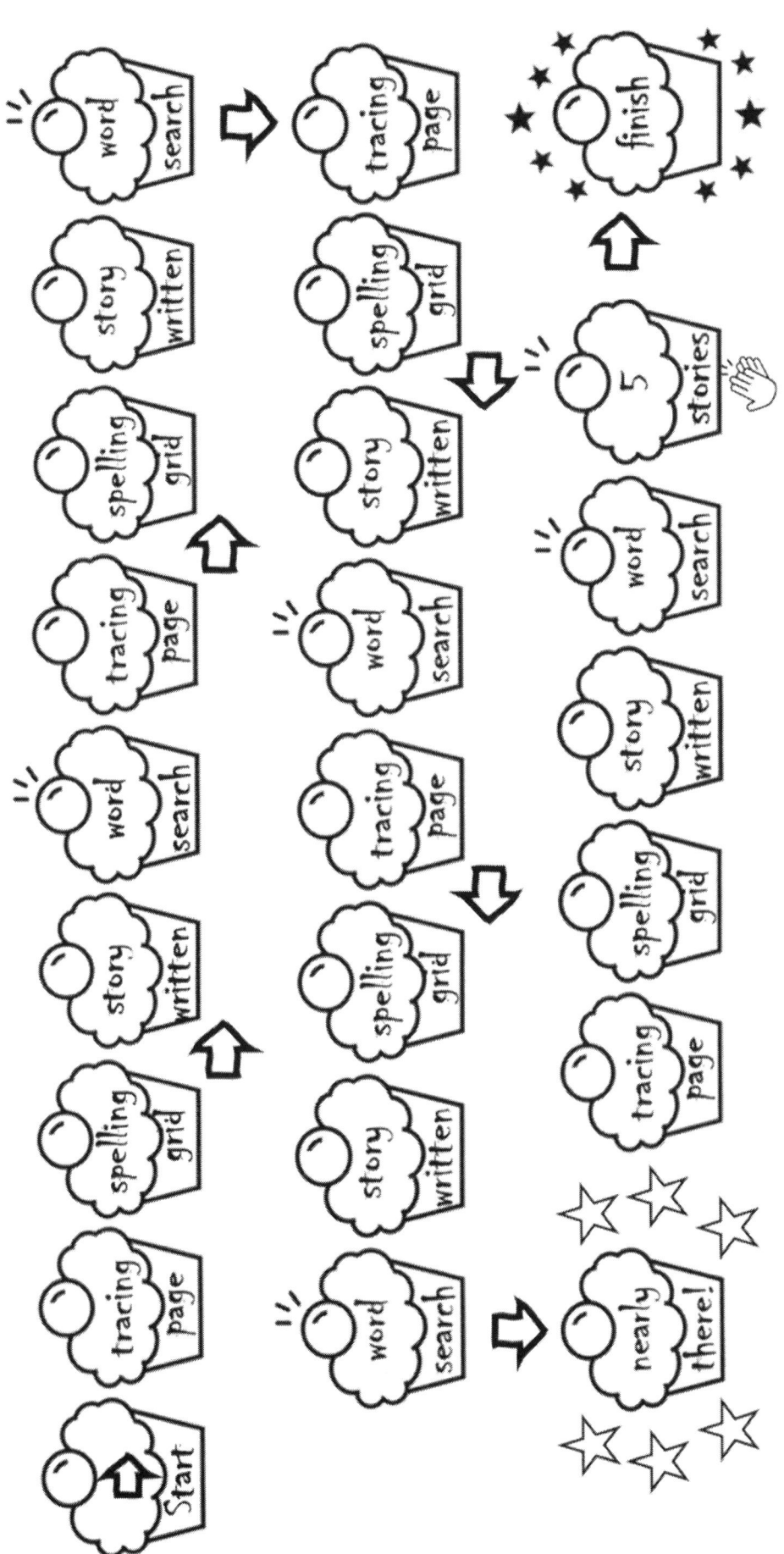

**Reward Chart:** Colour in a cupcake for each task you complete for stories 1-5!

# The Best Snow Day Ever

**To prepare for writing your story:**

**Practise tracing the common exception words:**

*could could could could*

*door door door door*

*sure sure sure sure sure*

*any any any any*

*cold cold cold cold cold*

**Now write the two trickiest ones again:**

To prepare for writing your story:

Now practise writing the words in the spelling grid:

| Look/cover | Write | Write | Check |
|---|---|---|---|
| any | | | |
| cold | | | |
| could | | | |
| door | | | |
| sure | | | |

Are any of the words still tricky? Write them below:

_____

_____

Date: _____

Adventure 1:

# The Best Snow Day Ever

From the moment I woke up, I was sure it was not going to be an ordinary day. It might sound strange but I could just feel something interesting in the air. Wondering what it could be, I quickly opened the curtains and saw that the garden was covered in a blanket of thick, white snow. Just when I thought things couldn't actually get any better, my brother ran into my room to tell me that school was closed for a snow day! It was still early but we got up and ran out of the back door into the cold.          *Continue your story*          ➡

By: _____

# Design a book cover for your story:

## Words to find:

snow

any

cold

could

door

sure

| p | a | h | q | v | c | w |
|---|---|---|---|---|---|---|
| s | w | n | e | d | o | p |
| g | e | r | y | s | u | d |
| m | u | r | d | n | l | z |
| s | l | e | u | o | d | x |
| w | k | a | c | w | o | n |
| o | l | s | u | i | v | r |

## Words to colour:

cold

any

could

door

could

sure

cold

door

sure

any

# A Trip to the Circus

To prepare for writing your story:

Practise tracing the common exception words:

children                              children

floor    floor        floor    floor

class    class        class    class

move    move        move        move

last    last    last    last    last

Now write the two trickiest ones again:

To prepare for writing your story:

Now practise writing the words in the spelling grid:

| Look/cover | Write | Write | Check |
|---|---|---|---|
| children | | | |
| class | | | |
| floor | | | |
| last | | | |
| move | | | |

Are any of the words still tricky? Write them below:

_____

_____

Date: _____

Try to include:    floor      move

children    class      last

Adventure 2:

# A Trip to the Circus

The day of our trip to the circus was here at last! It was a cold day in February but luckily we had wrapped up warm. I was here with a group of children from my class and now here we all were, sitting in our seats and waiting for the action to start. I was so excited that I could hardly move! Then everything went dark apart from a spotlight that shone a small, yellow circle onto the floor in front of us. Out stepped the circus master and then the fun began.

*Continue your story* ⟶

By: _____

# Design a book cover for your story:

## Wordsearch

circus

children

class

floor

last

move

| | | | | | | | |
|---|---|---|---|---|---|---|---|
| u | z | l | c | a | e | c | g |
| y | e | c | l | g | r | h | z |
| y | u | i | a | y | i | i | f |
| h | r | r | s | q | m | l | l |
| j | i | c | s | d | o | d | o |
| z | q | u | k | j | v | r | o |
| l | a | s | t | r | e | e | r |
| o | n | v | i | c | r | n | a |

## Words to colour:

class    move    FLOOR

children    children    move

last

FLOOR    last    class

# A Walk in the Forest

**To prepare for writing your story:**

**Practise tracing the common exception words:**

*should should should*

*pretty pretty pretty*

*mind mind mind mind*

*past past past past past*

*old old old old old old*

**Now write the two trickiest ones again:**

# To prepare for writing your story:

Now practise writing the words in the spelling grid:

| Look/cover | Write | Write | Check |
|------------|-------|-------|-------|
| mind | | | |
| old | | | |
| past | | | |
| pretty | | | |
| should | | | |

Are any of the words still tricky? Write them below:

_____

_____

Date: _____

**Try to include:**  past    should

mind    old    pretty

Adventure 3:

# A Walk in the Forest

The sun was shining, the sky was blue and Emily was happily playing in the forest with her brother, Cole, while her family sat on a picnic blanket nearby. They skipped past a very old tree with a huge trunk and saw a rabbit with pretty, pink ears beckoning to them from the entrance to a tunnel. Should they follow the rabbit inside? "Mum and Dad will never mind us having an adventure, as long as we stick together," said Cole. Emily agreed and, holding Cole's hand, followed.                    *Continue your story*  ⟶

_____

_____

_____

_____

_____

_____

_____

_____

By: _____

# Design a book cover for your story:

## Wordsearch

forest

mind

old

past

pretty

should

| | | | | | | | |
|---|---|---|---|---|---|---|---|
| p | x | w | p | q | t | h | x |
| g | a | z | r | s | g | g | i |
| q | s | s | e | o | w | w | s |
| u | h | r | t | l | c | z | q |
| s | o | b | t | d | q | m | e |
| f | u | m | y | g | y | i | k |
| n | l | i | k | n | y | n | x |
| q | d | l | x | d | a | d | b |

## Words to colour:

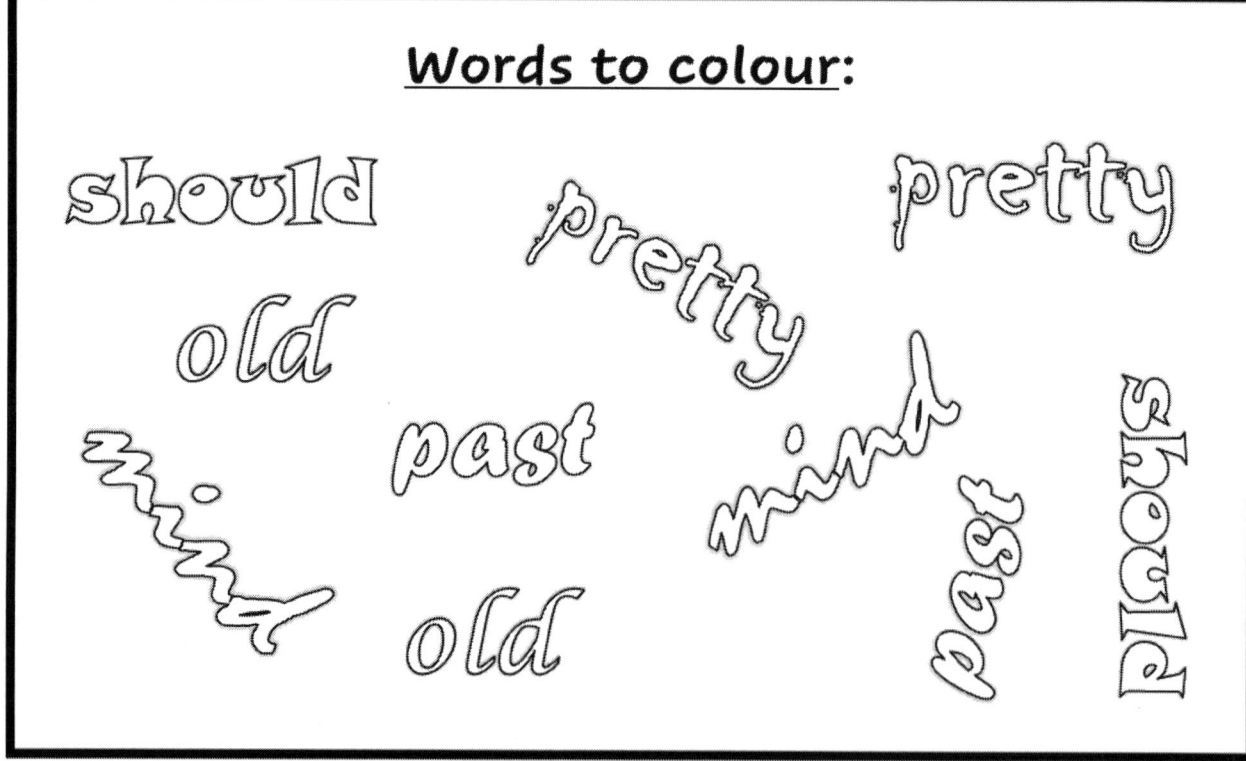

# Grandad's Greenhouse

To prepare for writing your story:

Practise tracing the common exception words:

again     again     again

plant     plant     plant

told     told     told     told

busy     busy     busy     busy

fast     fast     fast     fast     fast

Now write the two trickiest ones again:

To prepare for writing your story:

Now practise writing the words in the spelling grid:

| Look/cover | Write | Write | Check |
|------------|-------|-------|-------|
| again | | | |
| busy | | | |
| fast | | | |
| plant | | | |
| told | | | |

Are any of the words still tricky? Write them below:

_____

_____

Date: _____

Adventure 4:

## Grandad's Greenhouse

There was nothing Aisha liked more than helping in the garden and so when Grandad Jim told her he needed some help in the greenhouse, she could not get there fast enough. Aisha was busy planting seeds in pots when she thought she heard a voice. It wasn't Grandad Jim's voice. Had she imagined it? Just then she heard it again and spotted a little mouse in between the pots.

"Do you know where I might find some cheese?" asked the mouse in a squeaky but very polite voice.

*Continue your story* ➞

By: _____

# Design a book cover for your story:

## Wordsearch

grandad
again
busy
fast
plant
told

| t | g | r | a | n | d | a | d |
|---|---|---|---|---|---|---|---|
| w | o | t | x | m | s | g | b |
| z | p | l | a | n | t | a | f |
| o | z | j | d | s | t | i | v |
| a | w | u | a | h | a | n | b |
| j | h | f | z | q | a | t | u |
| o | w | c | h | f | q | n | s |
| l | x | z | y | k | a | e | y |

## Words to colour:

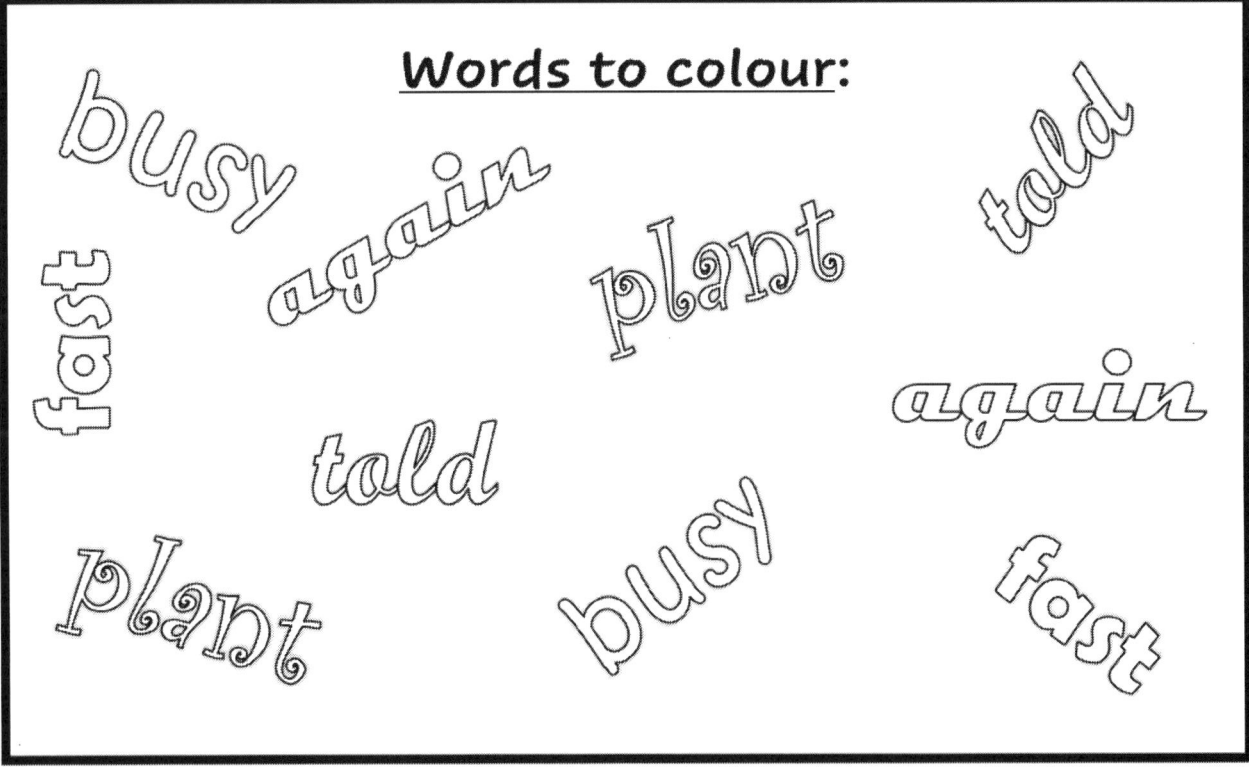

# A Day at the Water Park

## To prepare for writing your story:

## Practise tracing the common exception words:

*father* *father* *father*

*water* *water* *water*

*climb* *climb* *climb* *climb*

*grass* *grass* *grass* *grass*

*both* *both* *both* *both* *both*

## Now write the two trickiest ones again:

To prepare for writing your story:

Now practise writing the words in the spelling grid:

| Look/cover | Write | Write | Check |
|---|---|---|---|
| both | | | |
| climb | | | |
| father | | | |
| grass | | | |
| water | | | |

Are any of the words still tricky? Write them below:

_____

_____

Date: _____

Try to include: father water
both
climb grass

Adventure 5:

# A Day at the Water Park

My best friend, Scott, is so lucky because his father works at the water park and they always get free tickets. When Scott invited me to go there for the day, I was very excited. We arrived and found a place on the grass to put our picnic blanket and all our stuff. Then we changed into our swimming things and it was time for the fun to start! Scott and I went straight for the nearest slide and climbed up the steps at the back. When it was our turn, we both sat down and off we went.                    *Continue your story* ⟶

By: _____

# Design a book cover for your story:

## Wordsearch

- ticket
- both
- climb
- father
- grass
- water

| | | | | | | | |
|---|---|---|---|---|---|---|---|
| r | c | y | o | w | o | y | z |
| p | b | o | t | h | p | d | f |
| w | a | t | e | r | t | f | e |
| d | c | l | i | m | b | a | z |
| g | d | i | k | c | y | t | r |
| c | d | f | l | l | k | h | g |
| g | r | a | s | s | g | e | x |
| p | b | v | y | v | k | r | t |

## Words to colour:

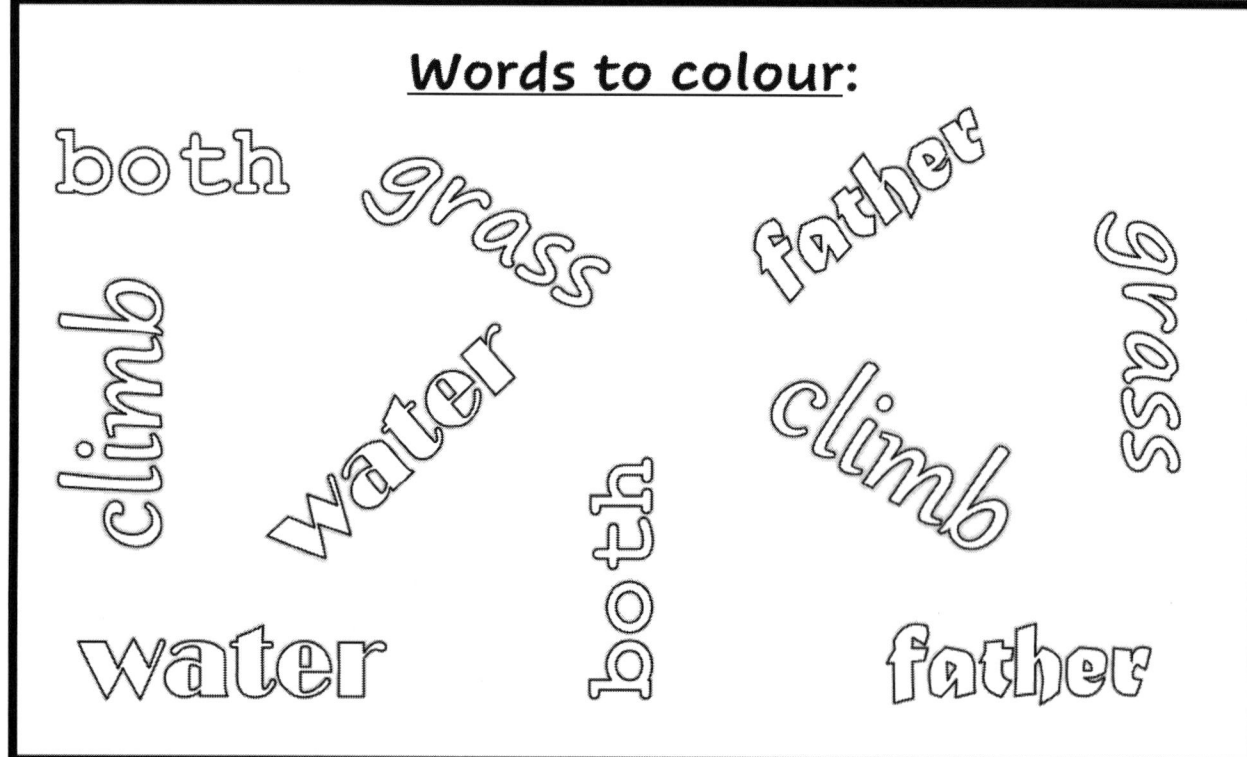

both   grass   father   grass

climb   water   climb

water   both   father

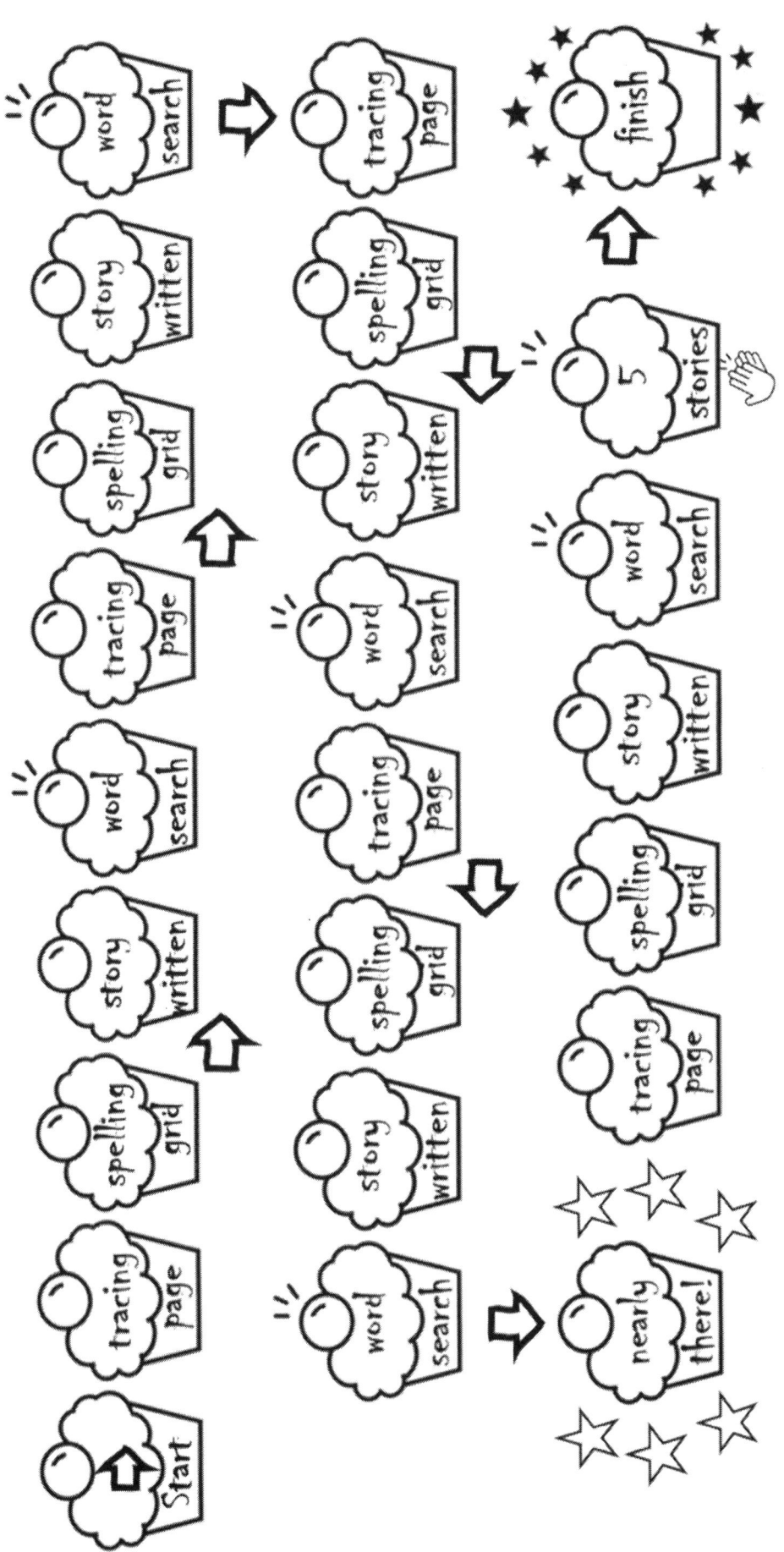

Reward Chart: Colour in a cupcake for each task you complete for stories 6-10!

# The Talking Tree

**To prepare for writing your story:**

**Practise tracing the common exception words:**

beautiful beautiful

people people people

again again again

told told told told

any any any any

**Now write the two trickiest ones again:**

To prepare for writing your story:

Now practise writing the words in the spelling grid:

| Look/cover | Write | Write | Check |
|---|---|---|---|
| again | | | |
| any | | | |
| beautiful | | | |
| people | | | |
| told | | | |

Are any of the words still tricky? Write them below:

_____

_____

Date: _____

Adventure 6:

# The Talking Tree

At the end of my Gran's garden was a beautiful

oak tree with a huge trunk and long branches

that were perfect for sitting on. Everybody told

me that it was a special tree but I didn't take

any notice of what people said about it. Then last

Sunday, I was sitting in the tree, watching the

autumn leaves falling to the ground, when I

suddenly heard the tree whisper my name! At first

I thought I must be dreaming but then I heard it

again. It was definitely the tree whispering my

name.                    *Continue your story* ➞

By: _____

# Design a book cover for your story:

## Wordsearch

- tree
- again
- any
- beautiful
- told
- people

```
g  b  q  t  o  l  d  h  h
h  e  a  l  r  p  p  z  v
c  a  g  n  d  e  q  m  h
x  u  a  f  y  o  e  i  t
u  t  i  y  m  p  s  p  g
p  i  n  b  s  l  o  c  v
u  f  l  o  b  e  h  y  a
t  u  d  m  r  i  r  p  b
v  l  e  l  u  c  f  b  t
```

## Words to colour:

again    told    people    any

beautiful    told    beautiful

any

people    again

# My Summer Holiday

## To prepare for writing your story:

Practise tracing the common exception words:

*beautiful*            *beautiful*

*would*      *would*      *would*

*whole*      *whole*      *whole*

*after*    *after*    *after*    *after*

*half half half half half*

## Now write the two trickiest ones again:

To prepare for writing your story:

Now practise writing the words in the spelling grid:

| Look/cover | Write | Write | Check |
|---|---|---|---|
| after | | | |
| beautiful | | | |
| half | | | |
| whole | | | |
| would | | | |

Are any of the words still tricky? Write them below:

_____

_____

Date: _____

Adventure 7:

# My Summer Holiday

At last the summer holidays were here and we started the long drive to the seaside, where we were going to stay for two whole weeks. After three and a half hours in the car, we finally arrived at our destination. Once we had unpacked everything, we got changed into our swimming things and made some sandwiches for a picnic. It would be hard to describe how beautiful the beach looked to me when I first saw it! I just couldn't wait and ran across the sand and jumped into the sea.        *Continue your story* ⟶

By: _____

# Design a book cover for your story:

## Wordsearch

summer
after
beautiful
half
whole
would

| m | b | v | z | t | t | c | r | q |
| h | e | a | m | o | k | p | o | b |
| u | a | u | n | k | h | z | a | h |
| v | u | l | w | w | a | q | h | f |
| e | t | q | f | h | f | o | k | r |
| z | i | n | b | o | t | m | k | i |
| d | f | i | e | l | e | j | k | r |
| s | u | m | m | e | r | s | v | l |
| e | l | l | w | o | u | l | d | d |

## Words to colour:

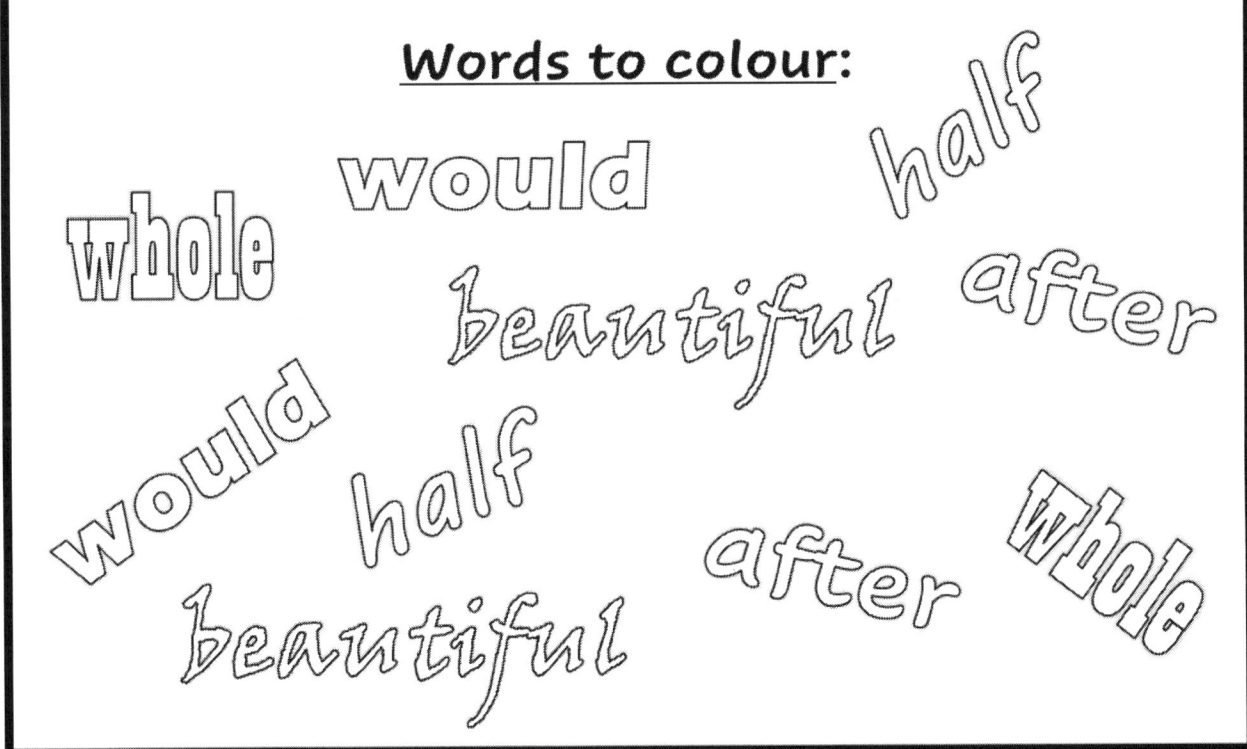

# The Friendly Robot

**To prepare for writing your story:**

**Practise tracing the common exception words:**

*behind    behind    behind*

*hour    hour    hour    hour*

*gold    gold    gold    gold*

*find    find    find    find*

*break    break    break    break*

**Now write the two trickiest ones again:**

To prepare for writing your story:

Now practise writing the words in the spelling grid:

| Look/cover | Write | Write | Check |
|------------|-------|-------|-------|
| behind     |       |       |       |
| break      |       |       |       |
| find       |       |       |       |
| gold       |       |       |       |
| hour       |       |       |       |

Are any of the words still tricky? Write them below:

Date: _____

**Try to include:**

find     hour

behind

break     gold

Adventure 8:

# The Friendly Robot

It was raining on Saturday when Joy and Jamie came round for a play date and so we decided to stay inside and play in my bedroom. After an hour of playing with Lego, we suddenly heard a loud tapping noise coming from behind the cupboard door. When we went to see what was there, we were very surprised to find a little, sliver robot with shiny, golden eyes smiling up at us. I picked him up carefully to make sure I didn't break him. "Hello," said the robot cheerfully. "What are your names?"     *Continue your story* ⟶

By: _____

# Design a book cover for your story:

## Wordsearch

- robot
- behind
- break
- find
- gold
- hour

| | | | | | | | |
|---|---|---|---|---|---|---|---|
| z | b | f | g | f | e | t | g |
| c | k | q | r | n | k | f | o |
| z | f | r | i | a | n | i | l |
| s | t | b | e | h | i | n | d |
| p | j | r | m | s | o | d | y |
| o | b | w | n | r | s | u | y |
| h | g | z | e | r | r | w | r |
| m | s | r | o | b | o | t | o |

## Words to colour:

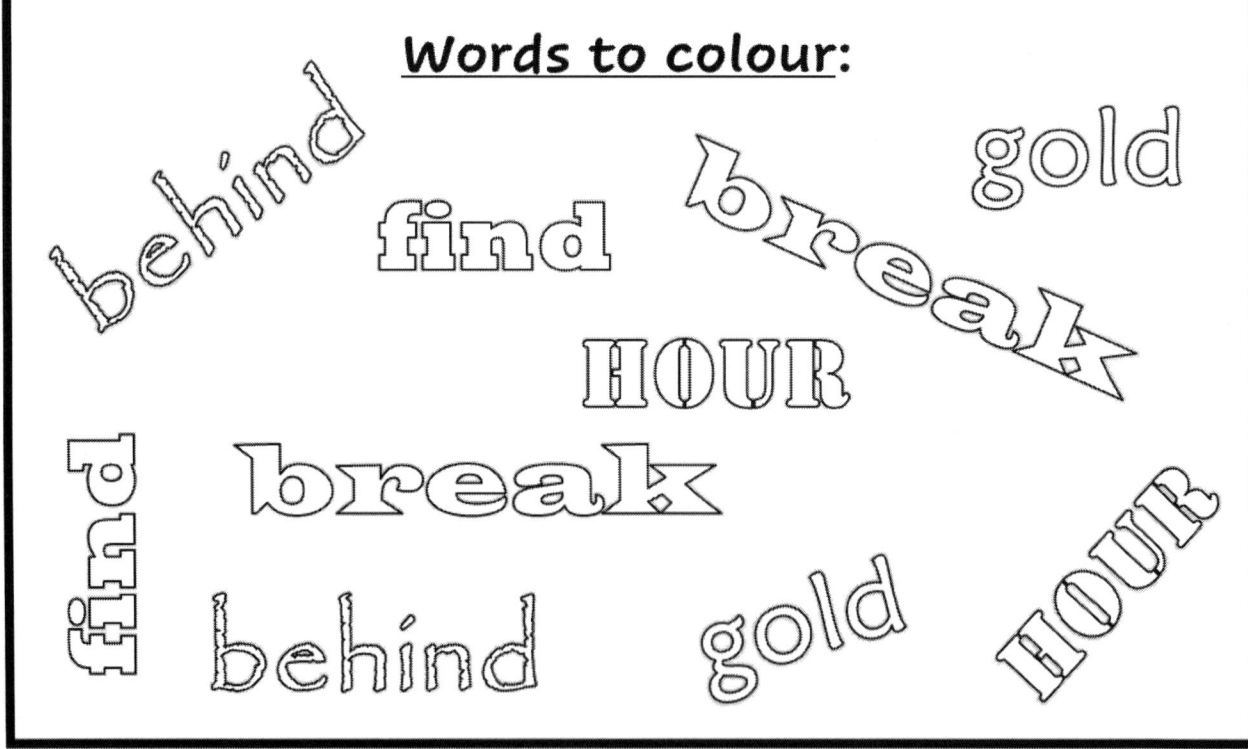

# A Naughty Dog

## To prepare for writing your story:

### Practise tracing the common exception words:

*everybody*      *everybody*

*steak*   *steak*   *steak*   *steak*

*most*   *most*   *most*   *most*

*bath*   *bath*   *bath*   *bath*

*wild*   *wild*   *wild*   *wild*

## Now write the two trickiest ones again:

To prepare for writing your story:

Now practise writing the words in the spelling grid:

| Look/cover | Write | Write | Check |
|---|---|---|---|
| bath | | | |
| everybody | | | |
| most | | | |
| steak | | | |
| wild | | | |

Are any of the words still tricky? Write them below:

_____

_____

Date: _____

Adventure 9:

# A Naughty Dog

Maggie's dog, Hamish, was small, white and fluffy with big, brown eyes. Everybody thought he was really cute and in fact he was very cute most of the time, but every now and then he would have a bit of a wild day. Like the time he jumped up and stole the steak from Dad's plate and went on to dig a huge hole in the middle of Mum's flower bed. Then he rolled in a muddy puddle and had to have a bath. Hamish saw the bath full of bubbles and refused to get in but Maggie knew just what to do. *Continue your story* ⟶

By: _____

# Design a book cover for your story:

## Wordsearch

naughty

bath

everybody

most

steak

wild

| b | s | t | e | a | l | f | r | j |
|---|---|---|---|---|---|---|---|---|
| s | n | t | v | i | u | t | n | l |
| i | a | e | e | m | v | o | k | k |
| s | u | z | r | a | d | t | x | d |
| m | g | y | y | l | k | k | l | o |
| y | h | m | b | v | j | i | h | p |
| c | t | x | o | a | w | e | h | c |
| i | y | w | d | s | t | j | a | d |
| n | l | i | y | c | t | h | s | e |

## Words to colour:

# Buried Treasure

## To prepare for writing your story:

## Practise tracing the common exception words:

*everybody*       *everybody*

*parents*   *parents*   *parents*

*find*   *find*   *find*   *find*

*path*   *path*   *path*   *path*

*phone*   *phone*   *phone*   *phone*

## Now write the two trickiest ones again:

To prepare for writing your story:

Now practise writing the words in the spelling grid:

| Look/cover | Write | Write | Check |
|---|---|---|---|
| everybody | | | |
| find | | | |
| parents | | | |
| path | | | |
| prove | | | |

Are any of the words still tricky? Write them below:

Date: _____

Try to include:

parents    prove

everybody

find

path

Adventure 10:

## Buried Treasure

Jane and Charlie were always digging at the beach, wanting to prove to everybody that there was treasure buried there. When they went with their parents to a beach they had never been to before, the children were overjoyed to have a chance of finding treasure somewhere new! As they walked down the path that led to the beach, they began to get more excited. Soon after they started digging, Jane saw something like a handle made of gold, glistening in the sun. What had they found?        *Continue your story* ⟶

By: _____

# Design a book cover for your story:

## Wordsearch

treasure
everybody
find
parents
path
prove

| | | | | | | | | |
|---|---|---|---|---|---|---|---|---|
| i | w | p | o | n | m | s | v | j |
| f | t | g | u | y | f | x | s | p |
| t | n | i | v | m | i | t | u | v |
| w | n | y | d | d | n | v | i | e |
| j | d | u | c | e | d | y | v | z |
| e | v | e | r | y | b | o | d | y |
| e | b | a | w | p | r | v | i | m |
| v | p | g | a | p | a | t | h | q |
| t | r | e | a | s | u | r | e | c |

## Words to colour:

everybody FIND prove prove

parents path

FIND parents

path everybody

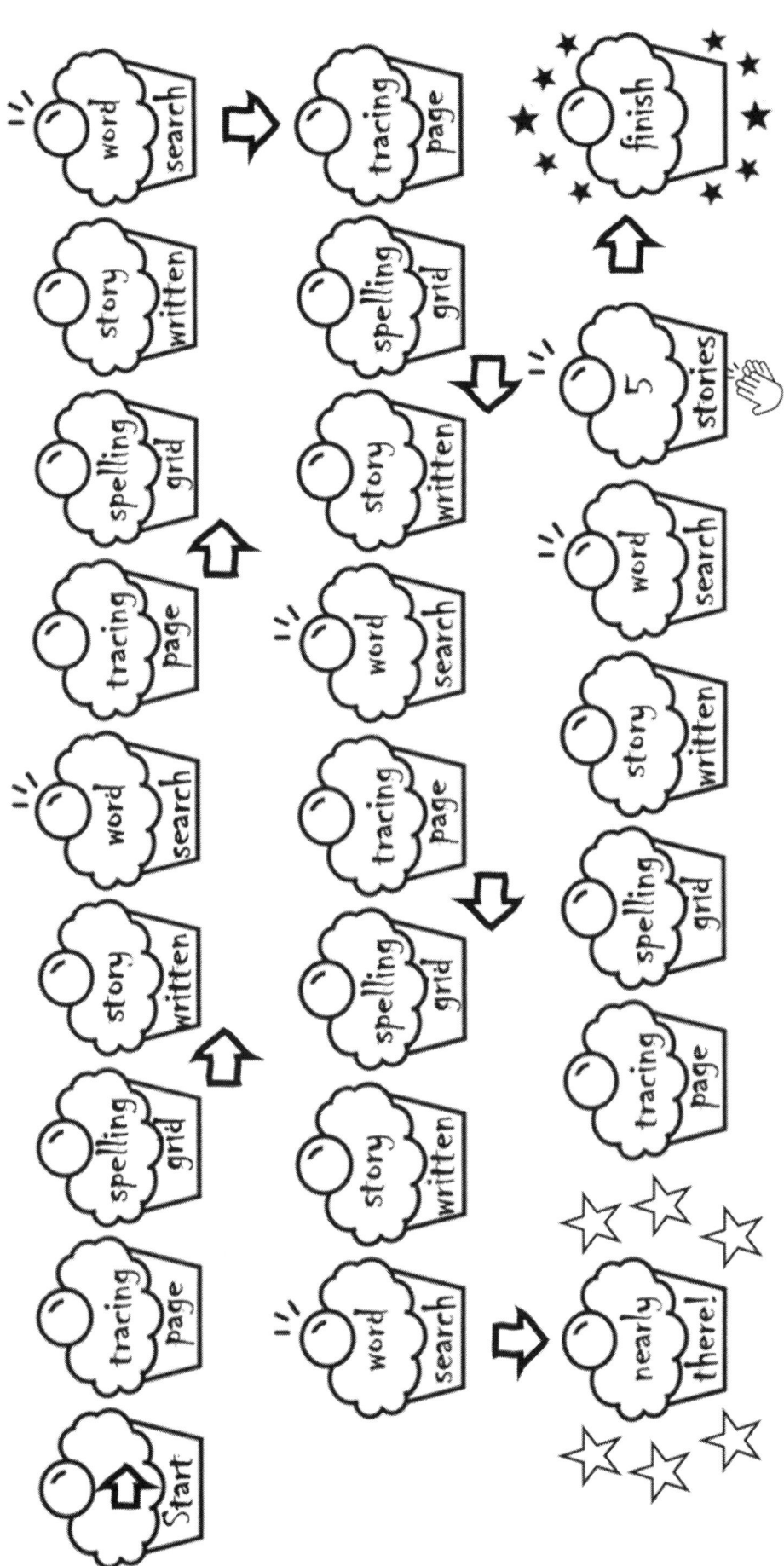

Reward Chart: Colour in a cupcake for each task you complete for stories 11-15!

# Tom's New Tree House

**To prepare for writing your story:**

**Practise tracing the common exception words:**

*great    great    great    great*

*poor    poor    poor    poor*

*hold    hold    hold    hold*

*Mrs    Mrs    Mrs    Mrs*

*pass    pass    pass    pass    pass*

**Now write the two trickiest ones again:**

To prepare for writing your story:

Now practise writing the words in the spelling grid:

| Look/cover | Write | Write | Check |
|------------|-------|-------|-------|
| great | | | |
| hold | | | |
| Mrs | | | |
| pass | | | |
| poor | | | |

Are any of the words still tricky? Write them below:

_____

_____

Date: _____

## Adventure 11:

# Tom's New Tree House

When Tom left for school on his birthday, Dad told him a great surprise would be waiting for him in the garden when he got home. As soon as Mrs Hussain opened the door at the end of the day, Tom took hold of his brother's hand and ran home as fast as he could. His poor brother was not used to running that fast! Back home, his dad passed him a key to a tree house that he had built while the boys were at school. Tom was speechless as he climbed the ladder to his very own tree house.    *Continue your story* ⟶

By: _____

# Design a book cover for your story:

## Wordsearch

- house
- great
- hold
- Mrs
- pass
- poor

| | | | | | | | |
|---|---|---|---|---|---|---|---|
| g | n | p | u | a | d | y | j |
| j | d | a | o | j | c | x | c |
| i | p | s | h | o | g | s | j |
| x | h | s | g | o | r | b | e |
| e | m | o | r | m | e | j | h |
| a | l | z | u | o | a | k | o |
| y | e | a | m | s | t | c | l |
| d | d | q | m | r | e | r | d |

## Words to colour:

Mrs    great    hold    pass

poor    Mrs    hold    poor

pass    great

# A Day in Candyland

To prepare for writing your story:

Practise tracing the common exception words:

people people people

sugar sugar sugar sugar

even even even even

kind kind kind kind

eyes eyes eyes eyes

Now write the two trickiest ones again:

To prepare for writing your story:

Now practise writing the words in the spelling grid:

| Look/cover | Write | Write | Check |
|---|---|---|---|
| even | | | |
| eyes | | | |
| kind | | | |
| people | | | |
| sugar | | | |

Are any of the words still tricky? Write them below:

_____

Date: _____

Adventure 12:

# A Day in Candyland

Penny and her cousin, Damo, were eating sweets in the garden when the shed in front of them started to glow and sparkle. When they opened the door and stepped inside, they couldn't believe their eyes. Everything they saw was made of sugar! There were sugar houses, sugar trees, sugar cars and even sugar boats on a sugar lake. All the people were wearing sugar clothes. A little, brown gingerbread man came to them and in a kind voice said, "Welcome to your Candyland adventure."                    *Continue your story* ⟶

By: _____

# Design a book cover for your story:

## Wordsearch

- **candy**
- **even**
- **eyes**
- **kind**
- **people**
- **sugar**

| | | | | | | | |
|---|---|---|---|---|---|---|---|
| i | k | p | s | u | g | a | r |
| d | c | e | c | a | n | d | y |
| m | q | o | j | n | o | r | r |
| s | j | p | m | i | f | j | j |
| a | e | l | n | e | i | z | p |
| e | y | e | s | a | x | j | y |
| s | v | b | l | o | w | d | a |
| e | k | i | n | d | z | g | l |

## Words to colour:

kind

sugar

people

even

kind

eyes

eyes

people

even

# Fun at the Park

**To prepare for writing your story:**

Practise tracing the common exception words:

*because    because    because*

*clothes    clothes    clothes*

*many    many    many*

*child    child    child    child*

*path    path    path    path*

**Now write the two trickiest ones again:**

## To prepare for writing your story:

Now practise writing the words in the spelling grid:

| Look/cover | Write | Write | Check |
|------------|-------|-------|-------|
| because | | | |
| child | | | |
| clothes | | | |
| many | | | |
| path | | | |

Are any of the words still tricky? Write them below:

_____

_____

Date: _____

Adventure 13:

## Fun at the Park

When she picked me up from school, Mum told me that we were going to go to the park on our way home. I quickly changed into my play clothes and we set off along the path. When we got there, I felt excited as I looked at all the fun things in front of me. I could see one child playing on the swings and two more who were already on the seesaw. I didn't know what to do first because there were so many things to choose from! I decided that I would start with a go on the slide.    *Continue your story* →

By: _____

# Design a book cover for your story:

## Wordsearch

- park
- because
- child
- clothes
- many
- path

```
b  e  r  p  b  s  p  k
q  e  c  j  k  w  a  m
x  a  c  p  d  m  t  a
f  l  c  a  y  x  h  n
n  p  h  r  u  e  x  y
n  w  i  k  z  s  k  x
x  c  l  o  t  h  e  s
r  l  d  l  u  n  w  f
```

## Words to colour:

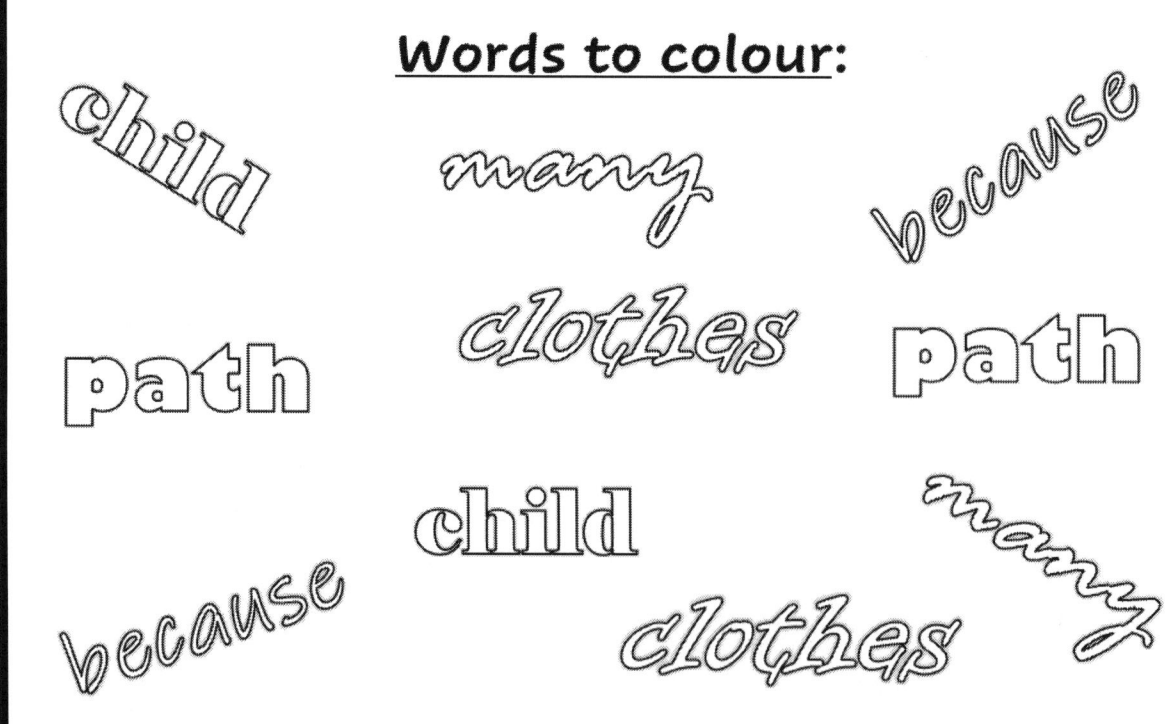

# The Magic Jigsaw

To prepare for writing your story:

Practise tracing the common exception words:

*improve*             *improve*

*money*    *money*    *money*

*only only only only*

*floor floor floor floor*

*last last last last last*

Now write the two trickiest ones again:

To prepare for writing your story:

Now practise writing the words in the spelling grid:

| Look/cover | Write | Write | Check |
|---|---|---|---|
| floor | | | |
| improve | | | |
| last | | | |
| money | | | |
| only | | | |

Are any of the words still tricky? Write them below:

Date: _____

Try to include: last only
floor improve money

Adventure 14:

## The Magic Jigsaw

Helen loved jigsaw puzzles and spent all her pocket money buying new ones. She did a jigsaw every day to improve her skills and now she had only one piece missing in the hardest jigsaw she'd ever tried. She picked up the last piece and as her hand got closer to the floor, she felt a warm glow coming from the puzzle and saw stars twinkling around her hand. Helen hesitated for a moment but then placed the final piece in the jigsaw puzzle and suddenly everything around her changed.                    *Continue your story* ⟶

By: _____

# Design a book cover for your story:

## Wordsearch

jigsaw
floor
improve
last
money
only

| | | | | | | | |
|---|---|---|---|---|---|---|---|
| d | i | m | p | r | o | v | e |
| f | l | o | o | r | p | n | e |
| l | e | k | j | n | i | q | c |
| j | p | w | i | b | e | b | e |
| m | r | j | g | o | l | y | r |
| u | d | h | s | n | s | d | o |
| n | q | s | a | l | a | s | t |
| p | m | d | w | y | v | a | q |

## Words to colour:

only   money   improve   floor

last

improve

floor   last   money   only

# The Lost Little Elf

To prepare for writing your story:

Practise tracing the common exception words:

Christmas          Christmas

parents parents parents

every every every every

who who who who who

Mr Mr Mr Mr Mr

Now write the two trickiest ones again:

To prepare for writing your story:

Now practise writing the words in the spelling grid:

| Look/cover | Write | Write | Check |
|---|---|---|---|
| Christmas | | | |
| every | | | |
| Mr | | | |
| parents | | | |
| who | | | |

Are any of the words still tricky? Write them below:

_____

Date: _____

Adventure 15:

# The Lost Little Elf

It was Christmas Eve and like every other child of his age, Alex was feeling excited. Alex and his parents had already hung their stockings up, ready for Santa who would be delivering presents while they were all asleep. Suddenly Alex noticed a purple mist coming out of the fireplace into the living room. Then there was a bang and he was amazed to see a little elf land on the carpet with a bump. "My name is Mr Humble. You must help me get back to Santa!" he cried, running over to Alex.                    *Continue your story* ⟶

By: _____

# Design a book cover for your story:

## Wordsearch

elf

Christmas

every

Mr

parents

who

| q | w | y | j | b | t | c | c | p |
|---|---|---|---|---|---|---|---|---|
| y | k | m | u | w | t | w | h | o |
| y | l | t | t | e | v | e | r | y |
| g | g | m | y | l | y | v | i | p |
| a | n | x | u | f | g | o | s | h |
| n | x | p | a | r | e | n | t | s |
| e | s | d | w | r | k | y | m | r |
| l | f | d | d | e | b | m | a | j |
| v | q | p | e | f | r | y | s | c |

## Words to colour:

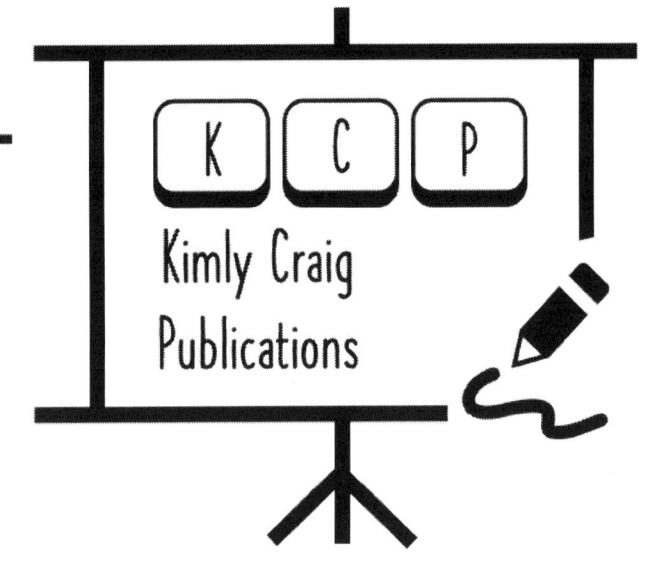

Kimly Craig
Publications

 kimly.craig.publications@gmail.com

 Certificate on its way!

To celebrate your child's achievement, email us their first name with a copy of their finished story and we will send back a personalised certificate to print out.

Write "Certificate" and your child's first name in the subject line and the certificate will be on its way!

Printed in Great Britain
by Amazon

11964002R00068